Wander

Wander

A compilation of my thoughts about life, nature and people expressed through poem.

by Rachel White

Copyright © 2021 Rachel White

Mildura, Australia

All rights reserved.

ISBN: 978-0-646-83476-4

Publication date: 22/02/2021

Imprint: Independently Published

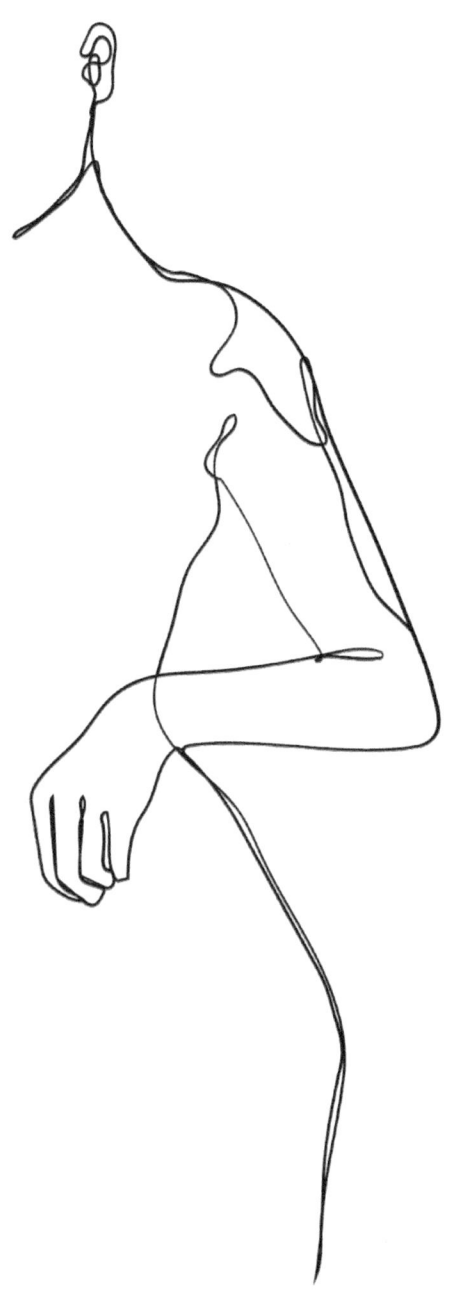

About the author

Rachel White is a coach for ambitious women who desire to bring their creative ideas to life, tap deeper into their intuition and lead the impact they want to make. Rachel is also an author, speaker and the founder of the Spirited Leaders brand including the podcast and virtual magazine.

Connect with Rachel
@byrachelwhite on social media
www.byrachelwhite.com

Preface

This book in a compilation of thoughts that wander through my mind, I felt an urge to express each of them through rhymes with some imperfections messed in.

Unlike my other books or public expressions, this compilation contains my thoughts in some of my lower emotional points and darker times. Usually, I would seek solitude in those moments, feel my feels and come back out into the world when I nurtured myself back to a more palatable state. Like all feelings are temporary and all moments fleeting, so too were the things I wrote about. They all represent single moments of my awareness.

Most of these poems took me less than fifteen minutes to write, some days I would three or five, they kept pouring out at times, sometimes a few days would pass without any writing.

There are many ways I could have shared the content inside of these pages, this was the expression and the art my soul craved to make. I am by no means a professional poet, these are the first poems I have wrote since high school, but I am all here for the magic and the mess of what poured out of me onto these pages.

Writing this book was for me, a way that I needed to process and untangle my thoughts inside my own mind. My hope in sharing this compilation of those thoughts is that they put words to what you have been contemplating or feeling or that your own creative expression feels activated.

This is your full permission slip to give expression to your creative energy, even if it is just for you. Allow all the magic and all the mess and everything in between.

Enjoy this journey as you wander through my mind.

Dedication

This book is dedicated to Emily, forever young in our minds, and to all the dreamers and believers who wear their hearts on their sleeve. Your emotions, expressions and creations are sacred and beautiful.

Poems

Emotions
Anger is a gift	16
Forgiveness	18
Love	21
Peace	23
Waves	25

Inner world
My deep dark desire	28
How lonely it can be	30
Tears	33
Shaken	35
Expression	37
Inner garden	39
Time is an illusion	41
Afraid to see	43
Lifting the veil	45
Boundaries	47

Nature
Waterfall	51
Fire	53
Water	55
Earth	57
Air	59

People
Emily	63
Lara	65
5	67
Nonna	69
Poppy	71
Antonio	73

Making love with life
Play with potential	77
Making a baby with the universe	79
You are the perfect amount	81
Goodbye to the bare minimum	83
Stand instead of reaching	85
Surrender to the crumbling	87
Your intuition is calling you	89
When life turns you on	91

Final words   93

Let's go for a wander.

Emotions.

Anger is a gift

Don't be afraid of your anger
This emotion is a gift
Anger is here to guide you
When something is a rift
When others treat you poorly
Or injustices arise
Anger builds inside you
Sometimes it's in disguise
It may appear as sadness
Or to others a surprise
But know it is here for you
Is it time to rise?

Anger shows your passions
A fire you have inside
This anger that's inside you
It's time to let it out
Channel it into action
It's ok to scream and shout
Then harness your anger wisely
Let your passion lead the way
You will make the world a better place
When you say what you need to say.

It is time to stand in your fullness
Honouring all this is inside
This includes your passionate anger
It can no longer bear to hide
Others may meet your anger poorly
That burden is not yours to bear
You can make the world a better place
When you show that you care.

For that you need your anger
This beautiful gift that's yours
Embrace all that you are
Let your anger open doors
The doors to experience yourself
In a new exciting way
Open up and scream
"MY ANGER IS HERE TO STAY."

I may not always feel my anger
Yet somehow I know it to be there
When it builds again I feel it
That's how I know I care.

I embrace my full self freely
My anger is a gift
I do not settle for mistreatment
Thank you anger for showing me this.

Forgiveness

I know that it hurt
And just how deep it cut
The betrayal and the judgement
Leaving a heaviness in your gut.

What has this turned into
And is it really serving you?
To taste the bitterness of resentment
All the heaviness in your body too.

Keeping this cord attached to them
While they likely have no idea
It is only harming you my love
Let's alchemise this fear.

The fear of letting go
To forgive what they have done
It does not mean that it was ok
It does not mean that they have won.

Sometimes it can feel easier
To grip tightly to the pain
But this is not serving you at all
On this path there is nothing left to gain.

It may allow you to feel justified
In the reactive action you take
Acting out from the pain
And the scenes you may make.

Are you willing to forgive
To give yourself this gift
To free up the flow of your life force
To mend your internal rift.

First you can be expressive
The pain you are safe to feel
Shake, dance, move and scream
The pain in your body is very real.

But the pain doesn't have to stay there
Poisoning you from inside
To transcend requires your forgiveness
Allow heaviness to wash away with the tide.

Forgiveness is an act of love
Love that is yours for you
It is not always easy to forgive
But trust this you will get through.

Love

What is love?
Is it something we feel?
Or something we are?
So many layers to peel.

What is love?
Can love been seen?
Is love simple or complex
or something in between?

What is love?
Is it something we search for and find?
Or can we never understand
Through the lens of our mind?

Is love always here?
Or does it come from within?
Something we generate
For the love to begin.

We know when we feel it
Or do we really?
It's in the little moments
That we hold dearly.

Love is all around
This is what I believe
I believe love fuels us
Even when we cannot see.

Love is here
Love is everywhere
Are you open to feeling it?
This love that we share.

Peace

If I want world peace
It has to start with me
An internal peace felt
For those around to see.

One being at a time
World peace will be here
Just one soul at a time
Is this peace near?

Only time will tell
Or can we have peace now
It can seem so far away
I won't throw in the towel.

I am committed to my peace
I know it inspires others
One person at a time
From our lovers to our mothers.

Waves

Sometimes the waves are gentle
A soft touch of joy
Sometimes the waves are rough
Crashing and loud noise
The waves are always moving
Through the high and low
Feelings so deep
So emotional.
The sea always in motion
The waves back and forth
Neutral ground in a single second
Before the waves come back around
When you surrender to the motion
That the ocean flows in
The waves all have purpose
No chaos or circus
Feel the waves move through
Move through your body
All temporary
All beautiful.

Inner world.

My deep dark desires

I have deep and dark desires
They are hidden in the shadows
Should they bring me shame?
What about me would they expose.

Some of these deep desires
That I judge myself for
I wonder if I am the only one
Who craves for them and more.

Some of my dark desires
I tried to let them go
Pretend I didn't yearn for them
I did not let this show.

One day I looked at my desires
The ones that are deep and dark
I invited them into the light
And admired their special spark.

When I could see them all clearly
I realized there was nothing to hide
My desires they excite me
My desires are a divine guide.

We all have our own desires
Do you play with yours?
Or do you try to hide them
Keep them behind closed doors.

Let's all shine light on our desires
In the dark is not where they need to stay
Let's normalize wanting what we want
Our desires are more than okay.

What previously brought me shame
I now claim them as mine
My deep and dark desires
With me they do align

The real me that is
Who knows not to hide
To be fully expressive
Excited and wide eyed.

I love my deep desires
My dark desires too
They make life more exciting
My desires I'll pursue.

How lonely it can be

Wouldn't it be nice
If we all just got along
Or is it naive to think
That we could all feel that we belong.

Could we all see each other
For who we really are
Understanding for all the differences
Seeing we all came from a star.

Sometimes I think to myself
That no one truly sees me
For all that I really am
How lonely it can be.

I do have loved ones near
And parts of me they see
But only what I show them
Why do I not feel free?

Free to show them all of me
The depth of my mind, body and soul
I give expressive glimpses
But I seldom lose control.

Maybe this is why
We all don't get along
Are we all hiding parts of ourselves
Pretending to be strong.

When really we crave to be seen
Or is this just me?
Am I the only one that wants to belong
So much and desperately?

Perhaps we are not all meant
To be in each others lives
My soul family they do see me
My love for me survives.

It would seem that my belonging
Has always been an inside job
I must first see me for me
My longing no longer does throb.

Tears

I was once a little girl
That cried all the time
Tears running down my face
Then treated like this was a crime.

My emotions were not welcome
In front of others or my home
I was a sensitive little girl
Who had to process my feelings all alone.

What I have since realized
Is that my tears are beautiful
They are not to be hidden
This is not disputable.

If your own daughter sheds tears
Or even your son
Hold the space they need from you
Instead of making them run.

It does not show strength to hide
Don't offer them cement in a tea spoon
Telling them to toughen up
Will not change their true tune.

It is not the time for tough love
That does not help at all
Not even a little bit
It only puts up a wall.

Show love to this child
Just like the love you once craved
It is time to end this cycle
Of hiding our tears away.

Shaken

My faith was deeply shaken
I felt fear all through my body to my core
A fear that kept me awake at night
Like nothing I had experienced before.

I felt I had lost my power
Like someone took it from me
I felt confused and violated
How did this come to be?

I thought I was in control
Then this control was taken and I was lost
Or was the control never really there
My boundaries they felt crossed.

What was happening to me
It still doesn't make that much sense
The ground beneath my feet felt unstable
I was in the open with no defense.

But my power it is mine
So I took all of it back
Trusted the protection all around me
With it nothing could attack.

Even though I felt shaken
The ground began to form again
I stood tall in my power
Feeling strong only then.

Only when I made the decision
The decision to stand tall
And own all of my power
It was never lost after all.

Expression

This is your invitation
To be expressive from your soul
To let us all see within you
All the beauty that you hold.

Be yourself, your full self now
For now is all there is
Don't wait to get it right
Your life is not a 'quiz'

There will be no grading
Only how you feel
Embrace your own self-sourcing
That is what is real.

Don't wait to feel accepted
That feeling comes from within
Don't let other people
Get under your beautiful skin.

You deserve to be expressive
To feel like who you are
To be admired daily
Up close and from afar.

Your expression is needed
On this earth right now
Don't overthink your expression
Or worry thinking 'how?'

Follow what feels good to you
What makes you feel your best
Accept all the in-between as well
Even when you rest.

Inner garden

You are more creative
Than you could ever know
Born with seeds of potential
Are you willing to let them grow?

To grow they must be planted
The seeds inside of you
The potential you were born with
Mixed with your commitment too.

Water your garden with your thoughts
And your emotional feelings
Fertilize with your big vision
Your creations soon seedlings.

These seedlings sprout and grow
The more you water these plants
You create your inner landscape
So much magic in your life this grants.

You are the creator of your world
Everything you perceive and see
You decide what to let in and out
How magical do you allow your world to be?

Time is an illusion.

Time is an illusion
Constructed from our mind
The sun may rise and fall each day
But we define our experience of time.

How we experience time changes
Depending on what we do and who with
Some minutes last forever
While some days go by so quick.

We process our life in a line
A linear sequence of events
But what if the book was already written
For us to jump between the contents.

Many different timelines
Are available at once
Which one will we experience
Well that is up to us.

What if what we think now
Influences our past
Could we reexperience things?
Or make a single second last?

What if we are just acting out
A picture in the sky
Frame by frame telling a story
Or is that just a lie?

What if there is simple bliss
In never really knowing the truth
In living in each moment now
Soaking up each moment of youth.

Afraid to see.

I was afraid to close my eyes
So scared of what I would see
I was afraid to fall asleep
Leaving my body unarmed while I dream.

I was afraid to look in mirrors
To see a reflection staring back
No matter if my eyes were open or closed
I felt like I was under attack.

I was afraid to close my eyes
I was afraid to open them in the night
I was afraid to turn corners
Afraid what I would see with my sight.

I didn't know what I was afraid of
I just wanted to close my eyes
But what I saw in my mind was worse
There was nowhere for me to hide.

I was afraid with open doors
I was afraid in open space
I was afraid I could just disappear
Leave in the night without a trace.

I was afraid of what was lurking
I didn't want to see
So I closed my eyes but still was scared
No place was safe to me.

Lifting the veil

I lift up the veil
And what do I see
My true magnetic essence
Staring back at me.

She was within me all along
Patient just below the surface
I just had to unveil her
To reconnect with my purpose.

My purpose can only be felt
Not understood or seen
It has nothing to do with what I do
Rather who I am being.

Boundaries

It was me who drew this line
It was you who tried to push past
Let's be clear so there are no mistakes
My boundaries are here to last.

My boundaries are for my safety
For my energy and my life force
For vision that is so important
And for my mission that came from Source.

You do not need to understand them
And I am not responsible for your reaction
But I do still hope you understand
And honor my boundaries with compassion.

Nature.

Waterfall

Nature is so magical I think
As I admire this waterfall
The earth so sturdy in structure
The water flowing through it all.
The trees, the sun, and air
In nature there is much polarity
Gifting us so many lessons about life
I am so grateful for the lessons I see.

Where the earth and water meet
There is luscious green growing
All the elements came together
The beauty of it is showing.
In this moment there is a rainbow
Shining through the water softly
The sun shining through gently
The rainbow to disappear shortly.

For a waterfall to form
Some of the earth erodes and crumbles
Forming an edge for the water to fall
At first there may be trembles
The earth becomes sturdy again
And the water flows over to the ground
Creating a scene to be admired
The earth again formed sound.

Fire

Sit in the fire
Feel the flames
Burn to ashes
Arise again
Feel to heal
Burn away
Arise again
Here to stay
Emerge stronger
Than before
You are stronger
Of this I am sure
Don't avoid it
This is your path
To feel the fire
Breathe, relax.
The flames burn
You will survive
Grow thicker skin
Survive each time
Your skin is thick
Your heart is soft
You are open
Even after
You were burnt
You rise victorious
From the flames
You sat in the fire
You were reborn
Again.

Water

Sink into the water
You are safe to
Surrender deeper
The water has you
As you are swallowed
Into water's depth
You are cleansed
You are nurtured
Nothing to defend
Nothing to prove
The water, it loves you
Surrender deeper
Nothing else to do
The surface has chaos
The depth is calm
Space to breath
Into the ocean's arms
The gentle movement
Becomes completely still
Can you surrender deeper
With your own will?
The water within you
It is strong and soft
Huge waves
Movement never stops
Or can it become still
Just like you are
When you surrender
To the depth
From within and afar.

Earth

The ground is solid
Beneath our feet
Standing on the earth
Soaking up the heat.
Burning at the core
Fueling all life
The earth is magical
In the day and night.
Earth expresses
In many ways
The desert, the rainforest
Each part beauty conveys.

Air

We cannot see you
But we know you to be there
The wind through the trees
The wind through my hair.
The oxygen we breath
We feel you in our lungs
When we are short of breath
The air it always comes.
You create movement
You create flow
Where do you start from
And where do you go?
Air we cannot see
But we know it to be here
Even if we cannot see
We feel it always near.

People.

Emily

This is a poem about Emily
Her life was taken so soon
But her impact was far and wide
Her laugh a unique tune.

She had dreams and so much potential
But she also had some doubt
We worked together to transcend this
Soon she was ready to shout.

To shout the message she had
The message she craved to share
To help other people boldly
For others she had such deep care.

She put everything in place
Ready to soon to begin
Her new venture to deepen her impact
Expressing her fire from within.

And then her life was taken
Quick and suddenly
It's not fair I often think
Her potential we never got to fully see.

But she did make a massive impact
With her energy and smile
And all the work she already did
And her unique expressive style.

Her energy still remains on this earth
Even though she is gone
From all the lives she touched and impacted
Her memory will continue to live on.

Lara

I met this little peanut
Who had big heart and dreams
She had so much to give
Her radiance, it beams

She made the decision to be brave
Her face and voice on show
The bravery sure did pay off
Into a walnut she did grow

And now she makes a difference
Each and every day
From what she shares and celebrates
To everything she has to say

This brave walnut is a snack
The tastiest of kinds
She demonstrates body love
Her example in many other's minds

This walnut's name is Lara
I love her to the moon
So grateful we have crossed paths
I hope we meet in person soon.

5

There are five of us
My siblings and me
Growing up together
In our big family.

The oldest is my brother
He likes comics and games
And building all kinds of things
He is serious or so he claims.

Next there is me
In my siblings of five
The oldest of the girls
And that first that could drive.

Now there is my first sister
She was confident and loud
Growing up together
She stood out from the crowd.

My next sister came soon after
She was always playing outside
She loved a builder called bob
She was checky and wide eyed.

My youngest sister came much later
The baby and cutest little thing
She loved giving hugs and kisses
So much happiness she did bring.

Now we are all grown up
So different from when we were small
But still the same also
My siblings I do love them all.

Nonna

My Nonna's eyes have seen so much
Looking from her kind and gracious view
Always looking for the beautiful side
In all that she has been through.

My Nonna's hands have worked so hard
But she never did complain
She is a woman that shows up in her strength
Whether in sun, wind or rain.

My Nonna's legs are short and small
But don't let her size fool you
She is capable of doing so much
Is there anything she can't do?

My Nonna's mind is so creative
She puts things together quick
Whatever the problem is or may be
Up her sleeve she will have a trick.

My Nonna's heart is the biggest of all
So big, kind and caring
Her love is unconditional
Her compassion is so glaring.

Poppy

My Pop came to Australia
When he was just a young man
He came for the surf and beaches
Then moved to the dry inland.

A little while down the road
It came time for him to move in
With our family, his grandchildren
A new adventure to begin.

My Pop still loved swimming
The river we would often go
He would swim to the other side
He said we could only come when we grow.
We would drive there in his car
The brown one that we loved
Lucky our dog in the back as well
All of us in his car we shoved.

My Pop was also a builder
Building new things that we mention
He would build us anything we asked for
Including a cubbyhouse and home extension
On all his creations he left his signature
A drawing of a small New Zealand bird
A kiwi drawn in his unique way
This is how his mark was conferred.

When my Pop left us with no warning at all
It cut deeply and left great pain
We feel him here and think of him when near there are pelicans
Hearing his voice saying 'it can fit more in its beak than its belly-can'

Antonio

Our little baby boy
How sweet his smile is
How did we ever live
Before he came to exist.

His tiny little fingers
And tiny little toes
How can he be this cute
Nobody knows.

Who will he grow to be
What kind of man will he become
We will love him no matter what
Just like we love his mum.

Making love with life.

Play with potential

I am a sacred soul
Visiting earth to play
In this world of pleasure and pain
In my body I love to stay
In my mind there is magic also
My imagination is quite vivid
I travel to different worlds
New experiences I am gifted
In these new worlds I see potential
In that energy I play
Then I bring it back to my body
The place I love to stay
Before I come back down
The potential and I dance
Feeling so abundant
Lost in a divine trance
I play as I am infinite
Desires all around
I see all of my potential
In my visions and their sounds
After I visit potential
I come home to my body
Anchoring all those feelings
It is time to embody
When I have come home
It is still safe to play
Vibrating at a new frequency
In the place that I stay.

Making a baby with the universe

Bringing creative ideas to life
Is much like making a baby
Coming together with the universe
Even if it sounds a little crazy.

First comes the flirting
Second you prepared the space
Third comes the conception
Then you start putting everything in place.

You can enjoy holding the idea
The energy just for you
It will soon be shared with the world
After you birth it when it is due.

There is no rush for the arrival
Of your magical creative ideas
When it is time your body will know
Until then your glow is to be revered.

After your idea is launched
Into the world it is birthed
Take care of yourself always
Call in your village and put you first.

Then you co-parent your creation
With the loving universe
Raising it through all its phases
In celebration you are submersed.

You are the perfect amount

You are not too short
You are not too tall
You are not too big
You are not too small.

You are not too quiet
You are not too loud
You are not too much
All of you is allowed.

You are the right amount
Of all that makes up you
There is nothing to change
Nothing at all to do.

Take up your space
You do not have to dim
Honor who you are
In the world you fit in.

You are not too much
You could never be
You were made just right
Look in the mirror and see.

You are the perfect amount
On every scale
All of you is perfect
Every single detail.

Goodbye to the bare minimum

Goodbye to the bare minimum
That only lets me survive
It is time to be open for more
All that I want to thrive.

Goodbye to just enough
I am deserving of more
I am worthy of abundance
I believe this at my core.

Goodbye to all that holds me back
From having all that I desire
I want more success and money
So success and money I acquire.

Goodbye to over giving
I am worthy to receive
Both in equal measure
Scarcity it's time to leave.

There is always enough
For all and you and me
There is no need to sacrifice
Not to any degree.

It is no selfish to desire
To have beyond your needs
Gratitude and desire can exist at once
No need for more good deeds.

We are both worthy now
To have what we care for
So goodbye to the bare minimum
You know where to find the door.

Stand instead of reaching

Reaching up to the stars
Stretching my arm and hand as far as I can
I want to reach so damn much
What is instead of reaching I just stand?

Trying to reach and grasp
Is only draining me
What I want so far away
That is what it seems.

Instead when I stand
I take my body with me
Using what I already have
Oh I feel the ease.

Surrender to the crumbling

Sometimes your crumbling is a blessing
Incredibly serving to your life
Everything falls apart within you
And cuts you deep like a knife.

All that no longer serves begins to fall away
Like an internal fire burning what you do not need anymore
Like the Phoenix you rise again
From the ashes you stand tall.

You may feel an urge to hold on
When everything begins to crumble down
To tighten your grip with all your strength
Holding on for dear life before you drown.

There is fire, there is water
And you have the earth to ground
Even if it feels shaky now
New foundations will soon be found.

When you surrender to the crumbling
Falling into the deep and dark abyss
You begin to shed your old identity
And enter into a flowing state of bliss.

The pain will not last forever
The light will shine again
Surrender to the crumble
You can be reborn only then.

The crumbling is a blessing
For you to be reborn
Anchoring deeper into your power
What no longer serves you is gone.

Your intuition is calling you

That feeling in your body
The pit in your gut
That could be a divine message
That you are in a rut.

That tingling in your toes
Whenever they come near
Is perhaps a sign
That you should steer clear.

Your body is always speaking
Do you hear its voice?
This is your intuition
Or are you ignoring it by choice?

You have access to divine guidance
Each and every day
For as long as you are in your body
Your intuition can lead the way.

Will you take this guidance
Or will you try to lead from your mind?
This mental path can only get you so far
Your intuition however is one of a kind.

Are you ready to listen?
Your intuition is calling you
When you practice hearing this
You trust what you have to do.

You are safe to answer this call
Forever and always, you are safe
Your intuition is your divine connection
This will always be the case.

When life turns you on

The experience of pleasure can be simple
Like when you are sipping a warm cup of tea
Or watching in awe as the sun goes down
You can feel pleasure when you allow yourself to simply be.

Pleasure is felt in your sacred body
It is through your senses you experience life
Are you denying yourself this pleasure?
Or can you feel it while it's still rife.

Let pleasure tingle in your body
In your chest and between your legs
Don't deny yourself this pleasure
Feel turned on till your body begs.

Begs for more and more
Oh yes right there
Exploring all parts of you
Next you are guided where.

When you get turned on by life
You become more magnetic
Attracting your desires
And launching a pleasure fueled epidemic.

Final Words

Thank you for being here
I hope you enjoyed my words
The wander you had through my mind
And the messages my words conferred.
These poems had to take this form
For me to fully express
Some may not make sense to you
Let your heart hear them first.

What wants to be expressed from you?
Trust me there is something there
Whether it is deep inside or at the surface
Be bold in expressing about what you care.

Take your first step
Your body and heart will lead the way
If you let them that is
Express while keeping your mind at bay
Your mind may create doubt
That spirals into fear
That is how you know
A masterpiece is near.
Fear only comes to show you
What is for your expansion
Feel and take your first step
Soon your creative juice could fill a mansion.

Trust yourself as you create
Validate your value as you go
I cannot wait to see
Which creations with the world you show.

Write your own poem – full permission to be a little messy, full permission to be expressive of what is in your body and heart, and full permission for it to not even rhyme or be anywhere near perfect.

www.ingramcontent.com/pod-product-compliance
Lightning Source LLC
Chambersburg PA
CBHW020328010526
44107CB00054B/2020